Reviews for

Starting Your Own Business - *The Fundamentals*

"Lin Wilder has put together a great guide to help you grasp the basics of beginning a new home based business venture. There is valuable information from inception, to completion. This book directs you in getting the initial set up, the tools you need to decide on from merchant accounts, to shopping carts and auto-responders, web traffic and lead generation, emailing, phone interviews, and closing sales. It is well written and easy to understand. If you are serious about beginning an on-line adventure, this book is a must have for you."

Lynn Leach
Lynn Leach Consulting

"I have been a business client of [Lins] for the past few months and find her capable, credible and compassionate towards her clients. Lin communicates clearly, concisely and with confidence in her book, *A Guide To Starting Your Own Business*; ...if you are searching, want or need guidance in starting your own business, become one of Lin's Marketing Lead Clients or E-zine Readers and you will find out that Lin is an honorable no nonsense professional marketer who says what she means and means what she says."

Carl Wasaff
Affiliate Marketer, Houston TX

"...If you are looking to start your own business you can't beat [*A Guide to Starting Your Own Business The Fundamentals* by Lin Wilder]. This book will open your eyes to ideas and guide you from start to finish [in] running a small business from home. [If] owning a business is something your looking [into] or maybe you've already tried but failed then this is a must read."

Casey Dean
Mobile, AL

"...Lin's Guide to *Starting your Own Business*...is easy to read...and easy to remember! ... There is something for everyone at different levels to learn."

Veronique Brito

"I love... *A Guide to Starting Your Own Business-The Fundamentals*. [Lin] covers all the bases well and supplies sources [where] we can receive additional information. The entire book is a wonderful testimony to the extensive research [she's] conducted over the years, and...the Social Media Tips adds tremendous value to today's marketing...I will benefit from it, along with countless others."

Roy

Starting Your Own Business
THE FUNDAMENTALS

DR. LIN WILDER

A Guide to Starting Your Own Business
The Fundamentals
by Lin Wilder, DrPH
Copyright © 2013

All rights reserved
First Print Edition 2013

ISBN: 978-1494464387

No part of this publication can be reproduced or transmitted in any form or by any means, electronic or mechanical, without permission in writing from THE AUTHOR or the Publisher.

Order additional copies of this book and other resources by Lin Wilder online at: www.amazon.com/Dr.-Lin-Wilder/e/B007L380OM/

Follow Lin Wilder at:

LinWilder.com
FastMLMLeads.com
Lleads.com

Cover Design by Suzanne Fyhrie Parrott
Formatted for Publication by First Steps Publishing Services

Graphics by Canstockphoto.com:
Pazhyna, (clock & money);
AnatolyM (3D people);

DISCLAIMER

There are no guarantees here.

I accept neither liability nor responsibility to any person or entity with respect to loss or damage including but not limited to special, incidental, consequential or other damages allegedly caused by any material contained in this book. We make no representation or warranty with respect to the accuracy, applicability, fitness or completeness of the contents of this program.

I do not warrant the effectiveness, performance or applicability of the sites listed here. All links are for information purposes only and are not warranted for content, accuracy or any other implied or explicit purpose.

I apologize for the inclusion of the above material. We include it due to the small but significant minority making such disclaimers necessary.

CONTENTS

INTRODUCTION
    The Time Money Ratio 9
    Team Leaders, Seth Godin and Steve Jobs 10
    What did Jobs do next?. 12

CHAPTER ONE
WHY DO YOU WANT TO DO AN ON-LINE BUSINESS? 14
    Let's start with the first thing; money is not enough. 14
    The second thing: If your focus is about how much you
    need to make money, you won't. 15
    The third thing: If you don't believe in what you are writing, selling or
    promoting, you will quit. 16

CHAPTER TWO
THE MECHANICS OF RUNNING A SMALL BUSINESS FROM HOME 18
    One or Three Caveats 18
    Ok, Let's Get To the Actual Mechanics. 19
    What types of professional expertise should you hire? 20
    A critical early step in your new business is your budget. 20
    What About Business Plans? 21

CHAPTER THREE
SELECTING THE RIGHT BUSINESS 22
    Find a business you really like… maybe even love 22
    Look for a business with a product people need. 23
    Spend time finding experts in the fields in which you lack knowledge. 24
    Create a budget and stick to it. 24
    Taking a Break 25

CHAPTER FOUR
GETTING STARTED. 26
    There is only so much busy work that we can do. 27

CHAPTER FIVE
AIM TO BE AN ENTREPRENEUR, NOT A ONETREPRENEUR 30

CHAPTER SIX
ESSENTIALS FOR YOUR TOOLBOX...33
    Merchant Gateway...33
    Shopping Cart...34
    Auto-Responder...35
    Blogging Platforms..36
    A Group of Favored Mentors..36
    A Schedule..37
    An Exercise Routine...37

CHAPTER SEVEN
LEADS...39
    How do we avoid becoming a victim
    of bad lead sources?..40
    Pyramid Objection Answered..41
    What do we need for the good lead category?...................41

CHAPTER EIGHT
BASICS OF TALKING WITH PROSPECTS...42
    Weak, "wishy washy" language...43

CHAPTER NINE
HANDLING OBJECTIONS AKA THE CLOSE...................................46
    Making the Process Complicated.......................................46
    I'm Not Selling...47
    Learning How to Sell..47
    If a prospect is not interested they will not expend the time or the energy to
    put up objections..48
    Summary...49

CHAPTER TEN
A WORD OR THREE ABOUT UNHAPPY CUSTOMERS........................50

CHAPTER ELEVEN
FUNDAMENTALS OF WRITING GOOD COPY 53
    Myths. 53
    Fourteen critical steps for writing "power" copy 54

CHAPTER TWELVE
Sounding Professional In your Emails 58
    Typographical errors. 58

CHAPTER THIRTEEN
DRIVING TRAFFIC TO YOUR SITE 61

CHAPTER FOURTEEN
CONVERTING TRAFFIC TO CUSTOMERS 64
    Finding Targeted Traffic 65

CHAPTER FIFTEEN
SUMMARY. 66

ABOUT DR. LIN WILDER 67

INTRODUCTION

One of the first things we hear when taking a look at the idea of network marketing is the ratio of time and money. For most of us, they are inversely proportional: if you have plenty of time then you don't have plenty of money and if you have plenty of money then you don't have enough time.

About fifteen years ago, I fell into the first category and worked a sixty to eighty hour workweek thinking it was normal. Yet, each day was a sprint.

To complicate things, little by little, there seemed to be less meaning in the job; office politics along with increasing budgetary pressures combined to make the weekends seem shorter and shorter. Monday morning would come in the blink of an eye.

The Time Money Ratio

On a lark one evening, I decided to check out a network marketing business mostly because I knew nothing about it and was curious about the idea of starting my own business. I wondered if it was something I could do…or even wanted to do. The person presenting was good, very good.

He focused more on what network marketing *wasn't* than what it was. It wasn't selling; it wasn't about stocking up on a lot of inventory that we didn't need-it was simply an on-line Sam's Club. Then he explained the commission structure simply enough so that anyone could understand it.

But what hooked me was when he began to talk about this idea of the time money ratio. Only rarely had I given any thought to the way I was *spending* my life, about the hours and days ticking by.

Ever thought about the fact that there is a limit to how much time we have in a day, in a week…in a life?

That did it for me. Not that I quit my job right then. But I began to dream about more balance, more time to go the things I **love to do**…was it possible? Could you have a reasonable income without hours in traffic?

Without having to dress in corporate-read-**expensive-**clothes or uniforms or whatever?

Fifteen years later, I can tell you clearly and honestly that it is not only possible but achievable. How can I say this? Simple—I did it.

Our life now is hardly recognizable when compared to the one we lived fifteen years ago. We moved across country and achieved our dream of life in a beautiful place and work on our own terms. Well almost…

So how did we get from *there* to *here*?

We decided to start…although we did not use the phrase, it sure fits; we began to "poke the box".

Just like so many entrepreneurs we've met along the way, we had to learn a lot about ourselves, our willingness to learn, to take criticism and to accept that since we were learning a great deal of new information, it was only natural that we'd fail at some things.

And we did.

Team Leaders, Seth Godin and Steve Jobs

Support, we have learned, comes in all forms: team members, family (once they recover from the shock of your decision, that is) and those who have gone before us.

Instead of reinventing the wheel, it's always a good thing to check out the experts. And an expert I tend to rely on a great deal is Seth Godin.

Seth began in the field of Internet marketing in the early nineties-when most of us didn't even know what the Internet was. Since then he has become a millionaire many times over.

One of Seth's latest books is titled *Poke the Box*. It is about initiative-about life without a boss or HR middle man or lawyer or…spouse telling you what you can or can't do-Godin knows how tough it is in this market-hundreds of thousands of jobs have gone to China or somewhere in Asia where they make what you make at a tenth of the price and yet…now I'm quoting:

"The intermediaries and agenda setters and investors are less important than they have ever been before. Last year, **sixty-seven** Web startups in San Francisco and New York were funded for what it costs Silicon Valley to fund a third of that number."

So what's the problem according to Godin?

Yeah, you guessed it: initiative-

Poke the Box, Godin explains, is a manifesto about **getting started** and he lists several imperatives to do so:

1. The first imperative is to be aware—aware of the market, of opportunities, of who you are.
2. The second imperative is to be educated, so you can understand what's around you.
3. The third imperative is to be connected, so you can be trusted as you engage.
4. The fourth imperative is to be consistent, so the system knows what to expect.
5. The fifth imperative is to build an asset, so you have something to sell.
6. The sixth imperative is to be productive, so you can be well priced.

But Godin claims that many of us, perhaps the majority, become expert at the 6 imperatives without ever reaching the seventh:

7. START; GO, "*Poke The Box.*"

If the last decade has taught us anything, it's that the maxim, "too big to fail" is completely-totally wrong.

So what is it that makes the difference between a Steve Jobs and all the Enron administrative officers who are in or barely escaped prison?

- Passion, willingness to risk.......and risk what?
- Failure -what's the worst that can happen? We start over...

Steve Jobs speaks eloquently about his career at a graduation address at Stanford University back in 2006-right after he had won his first battle with pancreatic cancer-it's an amazing speech and fits perfectly with the message in *Poke the Box*.

Jobs tells the Stanford grads that he believed he had no business speaking with them because he had **never finished college**-he was going to a really expensive school and had no idea what he wanted to do and felt as if he was wasting his adoptive parents money. So he quit after one semester and after some years of messing around, started Apple, grew it into a multi-million dollar company and then got fired by the man he had hired to be CEO!

What did Jobs do next?

He started another company, Next, then a third, Pixar and then back to Apple......right no college education just like Gates—www.ted.com/talks/steve_jobs_how_to_live_before_you_die.html will give you the entire speech and is well worth your five minutes.

When someone asks Seth Godin what he does, he says he "starts things"-most folks, according to Godin need a map-they need someone to tell them what the destination is and how fast they should travel to get there.

What do most of us do when lost? We'll travel in a circle while waiting for someone to come up with a map...is that what you're doing...waiting for someone's map?

Godin writes of computer people as folks who learn to "poke around"-they don't expect a rule or policy they simply write code, and if it doesn't work, change it and write new code....keep poking around until it works.....

Most of our culture-schools, the corporations and often even our families encourage conformity becoming very frightened when we step out of the crowd to do something different, to think differently or to live differently.

I wrote this book for folks like me who are toying with the idea of starting an on-line business but who simply can't get started for any one of a long list of reasons but who may get excited about the idea of poking around.

What you'll read in this book is based on fifteen years of experience in on-line marketing.

> I can't promise that you'll be making six figures within your first year
> or even your first ten years.

I can't promise that the transition from working for someone else to being the boss will be easy.

And I can't promise that you'll love working for yourself as much as we do.

I can promise that I'll give you the best tools I have.

And I do hope that you'll enjoy the read.

Wishing you peace and prosperity,

Lin

CHAPTER ONE
WHY DO YOU WANT TO DO AN ON-LINE BUSINESS?

I am sure you are thinking something like, "I cannot believe she has a chapter with this title? Or " "Come on, Lin, Give me a break, why the …does anyone want to start a business on-line or off? It's to make money, why else would I want to kill myself working weekends, nights and why on earth would I want to learn all kinds of stuff that may be hard for me?"

Or something along those lines, right? And I understand why you would think these thoughts, really I do. But here's the thing-actually three things:

- Money is not enough.
- Money is both simple and complicated.
- If you are not doing this because you honestly, truly, believe in what you are doing, you'll quit.

Let's start with the first thing; money is not enough.

I'd like to tell you a story about me and money that happened when I first began working on my home business in partnership with my husband John, so this was about 15 years ago. We had agreed that we needed to set goals for our new business. In our former careers, we'd both been extremely goal oriented so this was very familiar territory for me. We agreed to work on our goals individually and then compare them.

All went well until I looked at John's goal of making a million dollars within the time frame we had agreed upon, I don't remember now but I think it was five years which if I am right, we beat by three years. But that is beside my point here. John noticed my wordless stare and widened eyes at his million dollar goal and asked if I had disagreed with him.

A very long discussion ensued between him and me about the psychology of money-he is a psychologist so if he's qualified to counsel people, then it made sense that he could counsel me about money. I had felt overpaid for years in my job as a Hospital Director and in, a sense, felt embarrassed by the fact that I made so much money. I realized many things in that lengthy discussion, the most relevant to my story are three things:

- I did not feel worthy of making that kind of money.

- I was afraid that if that became a goal of mine, that I would join the ranks of people whom I had watched engage in behaviors I felt were unacceptable for me, like purchasing a 6000 square foot house for me and my dog, like buying absurdly expensive suits and shoes-that I would lose myself..

- And mostly, I didn't *need* to make a million dollars a year.

What I remember most about our discussion is not what my husband said to me but what he left for me to read after he headed out on an appointment. The article was by Mark Yarnell and what sticks with me all of these years later was his phrase: "No one person is worthy of being a millionaire." Yarnell stated that million dollar goals had to be about something bigger than you, something noble, something that sent chills down your back.

And so I got it and together, John and I discussed in great length what we would do with this money when we made it and whom we would help once we got there.

The second thing: If your focus is about how much you need to make money, you won't.

Right-if your only goal is to make money, you'll fail. I can almost promise you that. And if you can stop a minute or three and really think about what I am saying, then you'll understand why I say it. But I don't have the patience for you to tell me so I am going to jump ahead and tell you. Money is both simple and complicated, like a lot of axioms which are truth. It's simple because money is tangible, it can be measured, counted; it is what the world uses for payment, to measure success, to measure worth. But it is complicated because if you are so focused on making money that all you can think about is how little you have then I can assure you, the money *will* elude you.

Long before *The Secret* or the notions of abundance and scarcity were If you need to read more, a very wise man named Wallace Wattles took the time to write down some truths about desire, about the power inherent in formulating intentions, visualizations and about the power of our own minds in creating the world we live in. If you have never read *The Science of Getting Rich* by Wattles then take some time to download http://tinyurl.com/apcumgx. The hour maybe 2 that it will take to read through this remarkable little book will be well-worth your time. And then you'll see, I hope the rationale behind the fact that a desperate and single-minded focus on accumulating anything, whether it is money, health, success or peace will bring only its opposite.

The third thing: If you don't believe in what you are writing, selling or promoting, you will quit.

It's a funny thing, belief. We cannot touch it or measure it but we can *sense* it, in ourselves when it's there and most definitely when we sense it in others…in their confidence, the tone of their voice and in the way they carry themselves.

In his book, *Drive*, Pink quotes Mark Twain's *Tom Sawyer* to demonstrate what he calls the "Sawyer Effect." You remember that brilliant insight of Tom's when his friend Ben wanders by and sees Tom whitewashing then painting his aunt's fence? Instead of accepting Ben's offer to lose himself in self pity, Tom persuades Ben that painting Aunt Molly's fence isn't work at all, it's fun, in fact it's more fun than fishin'. Soon, Tom relegates himself to the role of supervisor while all his friends join Ben in the "privilege" of painting the fence.

Eminently readable, *Drive* offers both scientific and experiential evidence that the Type 1 person, most likely, you and I, find our rewards from the sheer joy of learning, of developing *mastery* or of solving a complex problem. Not that we work for free, of course, we want to get paid but money is not our primary motivator.

Like most things that I read and become excited about, it is because what I read affirms what I believe to be truth.

In decades of experience in hospitals, I was surrounded by Theory X colleagues and bosses. But there was a two year period where I had the privilege of working with a Type 1 CEO who knew that autonomy resulted in excellence. We took a hospital practically bankrupt and in less than two years turned the place around with a double digit million dollar profit. So the principles explained in Pink's book, *Drive*, are music to my ears.

Sound naive? Idealistic?

Why not test yourself now? Take Pink's Drive Survey to determine why you work full-time yet are spend your "off" hours working? Or if like me, you work full-time as an on-line entrepreneur, bet you'll test as a TypeI- *Dan Pink's Drive Survey (http://www.danpink.com/drive-survey.)*

So, take a minute now and reflect about why you are doing this…let go of the assumptions of the material world for a second or three and mentally list the reasons you're doing what you're doing, maybe even write them down for those inevitable times when you will want to throw your computer out the window or pull the phone out of the wall.

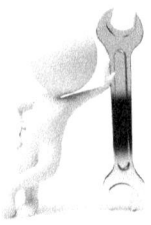

CHAPTER TWO

THE MECHANICS OF RUNNING A SMALL BUSINESS FROM HOME

One or Three Caveats

There is both good and bad news to becoming your own boss in a network marketing business. The good news far outweighs the bad but there are times that it doesn't feel that way.

Here is why.

Those of us who decide to work for ourselves have stepped outside of the box in a way that means we have decided to go it alone. There may be times that we look wistfully back at the old days of looking to someone else to create the vision and forge the paths for our life.

Becoming our own boss means that we are out there alone deciding on the direction and clearing our path free of thorns and underbrush. Often, it is our friends and family who test our commitment to go it alone. Although surveys repeatedly show that over ninety-five per cent of Americans are extremely dissatisfied with their jobs, most of us still consider the 9-5 job to be safer than the alternative of working for ourselves. So when one of us decides to take the risk of gaining control over our time and decide for ourselves what we are worth, it is usually those closest to us telling us that it can't be done or that we are fools to try.

Why is this true?

There are several reasons in my experience. The first is that those closest to us want to protect us from failure. Just as a parent with a child, they don't want us to get hurt.

That sounds like noble reasoning, right? Maybe and maybe not but let's start by assuming that they do have our best interests at heart.

Our friends may know the numbers. They are not pretty: 95 out of 100 new businesses fail. There are similar numbers in many other areas: over half of law school graduates fail the bar exam the first time, over 80 per cent of people who finish the coursework for their doctorate never complete the dissertation therefore can never claim the title. These are just a few examples of the discipline required of those with big goals.

And then again, those closest to us may have other reasons. For example, if your brother-in-law never took the risk of starting his own business, your decision to do so may be extremely threatening to him. Therefore, he makes fun of your "little business"; perhaps to you directly or to other members of your family. It is tough to handle this because our family members usually mask their real intentions under the guise of wanting to protect us.

But here is the critical question: what are the differences between the majority who fall short of reaching their life goals and those who fall flat on their face? You may look at the leaders in your company who earn extraordinary money and decide that their success is due to the superiority of their intelligence or speaking skills or their looks or their education.

These are never the reasons!

Experts writing of the differences between the people who reach their goals and those who fail are unanimous about the crucial characteristic: persistence. Successful people are no smarter than the ones who fail. They refuse to give up, even during the times when they want to quit more than anything else.

Ok, Let's Get To the Actual Mechanics

Business license, registration and domain registration are the very first steps a new business owner must take. Costs vary from state to state but you will usually be able to get your business off the ground and operational within ten to fourteen days of applying for your state license for $1000.00 or less.

Once you have your "DBA" from the state, you can open your business checking account, get checks printed in the name of your new business and get started.

Whether you should incorporate or do a limited liability corporation depends on the type of business you are starting, the state where you will do your business and the tax advantages afforded you if you incorporate.

Due to the economic downturn of the last several years, there are loans available from the government for small businesses and some banks are loosening up on their loan requirements for small businesses. For the majority of us who do our businesses on the internet however, the start-up costs are minimal and include only the basics: computer, printer and fax, telephone with long distance service at a good rate.

If your business is a virtual franchise or you are an affiliate, obtaining a domain name for your web site may be unnecessary although registering domains in your niche may be wise if you plan to write articles and or blogs, extremely useful in generating traffic for your website.

What types of professional expertise should you hire?

Unless you are an expert on the IRS, I strongly recommend the services of a good accountant who can get you started with a simple way to organize, record and report your expenses and profits. Most accounting firms also have bookkeepers if you can afford their services as well.

Most of us come into our home businesses from an institutional background where all the IRS, FICA and other fees were all automatically withheld and paid to the government. The first few times of doing the quarterly tax estimates required of all self-employed people can be overwhelming if you try to do it yourself.

You may read and hear from many experts that you must have a lawyer on contract for a new business and perhaps we have simply been fortunate but we have found that the fees of a lawyer are an unnecessary cost. We've been in internet marketing since 1997 and have never hired a lawyer.

A critical early step in your new business is your budget.

The number one reason that people fail in their new businesses is that they run out of money. When you create your budget, do be as thorough as you can possibly and include every expense you can think of. If this is not your forte, you may seek some assistance from someone who is good at this type of exercise; your accountant may be of help but remember, he or she will charge you for each hour they work; like you they are in business to make money. And then?

Stick to it.

Please, do not start your business because you are desperately in need of money. If that is the case and you are not prepared to invest money and time in your new venture, don't start it.

In the 15 years I have been working various types of on-line businesses, I have heard people tell me too many times that they **must** make their new business work, that their house will be foreclosed if they cannot make money within their first 30 to 60 days. There is a reason that you can claim your new business as a loss for your first three years. It will take your time and some of your money, not a lot if you stick to your budget, to begin to see your income build.

What About Business Plans?

I know that just about every expert will insist that every business owner must have a business plan; certainly if you are hoping for a bank loan, you will need a business plan and it will need to outline all the specifications you see when you research them on-line. But for those of us looking to work from home on the internet, I think it is a time waster.

Your initial goals should be simple and therefore easy to keep in your head: work to break even by carefully monitoring expenses and learning everything you can about how to sell your product.

CHAPTER THREE

SELECTING THE RIGHT BUSINESS

When making the decision about which on-line business fits you, it is wise to do some research before you join the business.

My five tips for those considering a new on-line business are deceptively simple.

1. Find a business you really like… maybe even love.
2. Look for a business with a product people need.
3. Spend time finding experts in the fields in which you lack knowledge.
4. Create a budget and stick to it.
5. If your business is not making you money despite the fact that you have thrown everything you have at it, quit.

Find a business you really like… maybe even love

If you are anything like me, there will be days that you will need to force yourself to work. Working from home is great in that you are your own boss and also bad that you are your own boss-there's no one to evaluate your performance therefore making it all too easy to tell yourself that the work you don't want to do can wait until tomorrow. Working with a business that you love makes it easier—a lot easier to force yourself to work, even when you don't want to.

How can you find a business you have passion for? When I started our on-line business, the only really viable businesses were network marketing or MLM businesses and there were over four thousand network marketing companies available to choose from. Fifteen years later, that number has tripled and there are many hundreds, perhaps thousands of affiliate on-line businesses to choose from. In addition, there are many on-line marketers who use their expertise to write newsletters and blogs in order to make extra income or to work on-line full-time as copy editors. Due to the explosion in E-Books and E-Readers, a whole new field of on-line experts in E-Book formatting, cover design and digital publishing, have come into existence within the last few years. Since my background is network marketing, that's what I'll discuss here.

So, what about **MLM or multilevel marketing or network marketing**? Is it a viable business or are they all liars and cheats? And are most of them even legal?

Yes, no and yes.

> "…The next time you meet someone who runs a "home business" or "MLM" give them a high five for taking their career and life into their own hands and becoming an entrepreneur," wrote Jody Coughlin in an article for Forbes Magazine.
>
> http://www.forbes.com/sites/chicceo/2012/09/27/is-mlm-a-bad-word/

So why the negativity, bad press and criticism that accompanies a decision to join an MLM business? Everyone has one among their close friends and or family-his name is probably not Ray but he's the guy who is the first to tell you what a stupid idea it is to attempt one of those dumb scams like an on-line business. He knows nothing about them, has never done much with his life, certainly not taken the risk that you have, of deciding to work for yourself, but that does not stop the dire certainty with which he predicts failure for your new venture. I wrote this several months ago in my blog, http://tinyurl.com/b5fc53w, *Broke Uncle Ray Is Alive and Well.*

And are there liars and cheats in MLM and network marketing companies? Well sure there are but unfortunately, we find liars and cheats in every walk of life, don't we?

Look for a business with a product people need.

The last time I counted, there were over 4000 network marketing companies-the number varies considerably because there are new companies launching and older companies failing but rest assured, there is a type and variety for you, if you look.

It's best to look for a product people need and will continually purchase: laundry soap, cosmetics, cell phone service, electricity, the more arcane companies may be tougher to keep people purchasing the products, the more exciting on-line businesses which promise high revenue but with products which are tough to define may be a harder sell.

Spend time finding experts in the fields in which you lack knowledge.

Unfortunately, there are many so-called experts who advertise themselves as having expertise but who not only don't know but don't know that they don't know. Network marketing and multilevel marketing has long had a bad name due to people who lie about what they have done and can do for you. They lie about their income, about the size of their down-lines, they lie about everything. We learned this the hard way, by believing people who turned out to be liars. Don't let that cause you to quit, simply recognize him or her for what she is not and go find someone who can truly help you.

The amount of new material, behaviors, skills and habits that you need to learn in order to succeed at any business is daunting—overwhelming in the beginning. Without making the decision to get command of the expertise you need, you will surely fail.

I began as a network marketer-something I knew absolutely nothing about—but I was drawn by the healing power of the amazing natural products; I witnessed the effects of the products in countless customers.

Looking back on those first few years, I know that we spent nowhere the time we should have to find experts or rather verified experts...Check out the claims of those whom you are considering to follow, make certain that you see evidence of income claims, don't be deceived by those with fake credentials.

Create a budget and stick to it.

Does this sound familiar? It should be, you just read this in the last chapter. This may be the most important thing you do to secure the life of your business.

Most people starting a new business will fail. You can check the numbers of those who succeed versus those who fail simply by researching the internet. Somewhere between sixty to eighty-five per cent of those beginning a new business will fail within the first five years.

Why? They run out of money. So know how critically important your budget is—treat it as the Bible of your business.

If your business is not making you money, despite the fact that you have thrown everything you have at it, quit.

Taking a Break

If you've been working long hours for weeks at a time and really, truly have been intensely focused on your business, schedule some time very soon to stop. Take a vacation-if not a physical one then a mental one and decide to take three days off doing what you absolutely love to do. You may find that leaving everything alone for a while has exciting consequences.

When you come back from your retreat, do an objective appraisal of your business: finances, customer list (is it growing or dropping), and honestly decide if this business is worth the energy you are investing in it.

Honestly ask yourself: Do I still love the writing, the web design and/or the work with customers?

> If you answer **yes**, decide how long you can afford to operate your business with the income you are making.
>
> If you answer **no**, consider searching for another business niche that will re-kindle your passion.

CHAPTER FOUR
GETTING STARTED

Seth Godin begins *Poke The Box*, one of his E-Books that I find worthy of returning to now and then with these phrases:

"This Is A Manifesto About Starting,

Starting a project, making a ruckus, taking what feels like a risk.

Not just' I'm starting to think about it' or 'We're going to meet on this' or…

No, starting.

Going beyond the point of no return.

Leaping.

Committing.

Making something happen."

Why does Godin stream together so many phrases like this? Because his book and much of his writing emphasizes his belief that most people don't really fail, they never get started. And getting started is the toughest thing to do.

Why?

There is only so much busy work that we can do.

If you reflect on the initial days and weeks of starting your first on line business, you can no doubt remember the flurry of activity. Deciding on what type of office chair, and desk, file cabinets and the like took some time and concentration.

The paperwork, registration for your DBA, business license and business bank account not to mention all the articles and research about whether to incorporate or do an LLC or not can consume huge quantities of time—and money, if you decide to pay for an lawyer to set up your corporation.

And if you did hire an attorney, no doubt he or she has advised you on the need for a business plan, one which will take even the fastest researcher and writer many hours to put together. But at some point, every detail that we can conceive of has been handled and here we sit in our offices, alone. And then what?

Then comes the doubt, the second guessing.

What was I thinking? I'm not a writer! I can't sell! I can't call strangers on the phone!

> I can't.

> I can't.

Assuming you've been doing your business for 6 weeks or more (less than 1 or 2 years), you probably have a mix of emotions about it right now: disappointment that it hasn't happened quicker, frustration with your up line, down line or both and a nagging worry that you'll fail.

You are likely getting more than a few questions from those friends and family members who have told you they will join you once you become successful.

And you are probably starting to worry about your answers to their questions and whether you are being truthful to them and to yourself when you answer them.

So when you talk with prospective prospects about your business, those doubts sometimes creep into your consciousness and when you think about why a prospect said no to you, you decide that it's your fault.

You weren't enthusiastic enough or you didn't answer that one objection right or your hair was a mess that day or any of a myriad of other self-critical assumptions. And you're both right and wrong.

You're right that you bear responsibility for their failure to join you but are most likely wrong about why. The real reason they say no is that they do *not* see what you see… (providing you still see it, that is.) Period.

I bet you've been to those yearly meetings where the highest earners in your company are asked to do hour-long trainings about what they did to get to where they make a fortune. Almost always, these leaders include their personal story about how they got to where they are.

Have you noticed the similarity to what each leader says when you listen to them? Not the mechanics of how and what they do when they prospect or how they inspire their down line, but what they say when they "talk from their heart" about the most important things this business has brought to them.

They all seem to say things like,"I am so grateful for what I have become," or " it is what I've learned and how I have changed that I value most," or "I'm here because of the people out there who put me here."

Do you notice when they tell their story like this, their voices change, they take on a passionate sincerity and fervor that is undeniably from their heart? They never say that it's the money or that it's because they are so smart. They talk as if they are now aware of something outside of them.

There is an Indian parable that goes like this: "If you thirst, the River comes to you, if you do not thirst, there is no river." Anyone who decides to excel needs to make a decision to do it; to let nothing stop him from achieving whatever his goal is.

Nothing. It's really a decision to have faith that the river: (success, a new life, completion of the degree, our new self, health, Truth, God)… **is** there before you see it… when no one else sees it but you.

Remember "Raiders of the Lost Ark" when Harrison Ford's father Sean Connery is dying and Harrison Ford takes the leap into naked space because he knows that he has to do that to save his father? And remember the bridge appears *after* he takes the first step?

Each of you has done that, at least once in your life; maybe with your kids, maybe with an ailing parent, with school, with a job or a football or basketball game that you decided to win. You took the step once or twice or maybe many times.

If you look back on that goal, you'll recall the obstacles that plagued you. In fact you can probably remember intricate details about those obstacles and how more fiercely determined each new one made you feel? Now, remember how you felt when you knew you'd made it? Or that you would make it? When you knew that you either were "there" or would get "there"?

Stick for a moment there, there was a certainty in you, almost an automaticity about the tasks that you now knew so well that you felt as if you'd tapped into something powerful outside of yourself.

That's what those leaders have learned, it's not about them; it's bigger, more powerful and they have become part of it. They did their part: the learning, the continuing to work through the times when they wanted to quit just like you did before you won the game or got that degree.

But they didn't quit so the River came to them. And it **is** still there but you have to believe it's there first-only then will you see it.

CHAPTER FIVE

AIM TO BE AN ENTREPRENEUR, NOT A ONETREPRENEUR

One of the tougher tasks for most of us is delegation. Whether the difficulty is due to a tendency toward perfectionism, lack of trust in the ability of others to do the job as well as we will, most of us resist trusting another to do the job as well as we would.

If your goals are, as management gurus liked to say, BHAG, or big, hairy and audacious goals, then learning the art of delegation is critical. One cannot run a large organization alone.

If in network marketing with a growing down-line, you are probably mentoring those who have big goals like you and if you have an affiliate business without messy down-lines, you must still get the word out via SEO, blogs, social media and the innumerable tasks involved in 21st century marketing.

None of us can become expert in all of the required fields; therefore the answer is, of course, to contract out the jobs in which you lack skill. The good news for the small business entrepreneur is that there are many places where one can find skilled people to hire for a single task or as a virtual employee.

Sites like Elance, Guru.com can provide freelance web designers, experts in SEO, blogging, copy writing or almost and task you can conceive of. And recently, Fiverr.com has come on board offering article spinning, web design, video production and an amazing variety of skilled people from all over the world; all for $5.00 per job.

Due to the emergence of technologies like Skype, VOIP, virtual assistants, (VA's) are becoming increasingly commonplace. Hourly rates for VA's can range from a low of less than a dollar per hour to over $12.00 here in the states.

Young and surprisingly skilled workers from the Philippines, India and China can make themselves invaluable in a very short period of time if you are willing to train and then delegate.

There are more than a few concerns with hiring an assistant who is hundreds or maybe thousands of miles away; these 5 rank among the highest:

- How do we know that this person can do what they say they can do?
- How can we know that this individual is really doing the work since we cannot watch him or her?
- If the VA is from another country, how can we communicate with her effectively?
- How can a stranger be trusted with credit card info and data base login?
- How do I determine what to delegate?

We began using virtual assistants from another country several months ago and had all of the worries listed above plus a whole lot more. But we knew that we were at a decision point and so we jumped in with both feet.

Quite frankly, the learning curve was fairly steep as we were not sure what we were getting ourselves into and we made some mistakes in the beginning. But here is a summary of our experience to date:

- Only rarely did we experience that an individual claiming to be proficient in an area turn out to be marginally competent. Our team currently consists of 9 people but we went through 30 to end up with 9 folks whom we trust. The problems among the 21 who did not make it ranged from inadequate skills to the painful realization that a young man whom we had considered to be one of our best employees had to be fired.
- Whether or not the person is actually doing the work or is simply claiming to do so is a concern for us, of course. But we have devised methods using Skype and on-line reporting mechanisms with which we feel fairly comfortable.
- One of our biggest surprises has been the English proficiency possessed by the majority of the VA's whom we have

interviewed. We have also found communication via Skype to be excellent.

- Trusting individuals with login information is something that we did slowly, very carefully and with some degree of apprehension but we have not had a problem to date.

- Because there is so much to do, we really did not have a problem assigning tasks but if you are not sure, these 2 articles may be of interest to you:

10 Things to Outsource to a Virtual Assistant http://www.entrepreneur.com/article/225318

and

7 Secrets for Outsourcing Effectively to Virtual Assistants http://www.startupnation.com/business-articles/9681/1/virtual-assistants-7-secrets-outsourcing.htm

After handing over the mundane tasks, a basic fear may be that we have too much time on our hands, too much time to think.

Psychologists have suggested that success may cause more stress that failure; the comfort of busywork prohibits those most critical of efforts for the entrepreneur: creative thinking, planning and strategizing.

CHAPTER SIX

ESSENTIALS FOR YOUR TOOLBOX

We have reviewed some of the basic requirements for your new business in Chapter Two, The Mechanics of Running A Small Business From Home but there are about five online virtual assists that you'll find useful if you will be selling products as an affiliate or you plan to create your own product(s).

Merchant Gateway

Shopping Cart

Auto Responder

Blogging Platform

A Group of Favored Mentors

A Schedule

An Exercise Routine

Merchant Gateway

There are many choices for your payment processor and the monthly fees vary from free to a fixed percentage based on total volume of sales, the number of fraudulent orders received and your credit history. You probably want to do some research before jumping in and signing up with the cheapest.

Here is a simple overview that is easy to read and offers really good information: http://www.ecommerce-guide.com/solutions/secure_pay/article.php/3869546/Buyers-Guide--Choosing-a-Payment-Gateway-Provider.htm

But you may not need all the bells and whistles provided by some of the higher priced merchant accounts; a simple account at PayPal may meet your needs more than adequately. Your decision should be based on the variety of your products, whether or not you will require a shopping cart as well as your budget.

Don't forget your budget, all of these on line tools are in business for the same reason that you are; to make money. In the beginning, you do need to be prepared to lose money. Most new businesses will operate in the red for a while but your very first goal should be to break even. You'll not do that if you don't keep track of all the small as well as the large monthly charges.

Shopping Cart

Once again, your first question must be, do I really need one?

Now that you've decided you really need a shopping cart, the next task is to choose one. As with the merchant gateway, the choices can be daunting and somewhat puzzling. There are a wide a wide variety of shopping carts along with just as wide a variety of costs.

There are some vendors who will claim that they are less expensive than their competition due to the absence of a start-up fee but then exceed the competition by doubling the monthly charge so examining the total fee structure is essential. This guide comparing 68 shopping carts for small businesses may be of help. http://smallbiztrends.com/2010/06/ecommerce-shopping-carts-small-business.html

Yeah, I know, 68 of them to research seems overwhelming and gives you a headache just thinking about it, right?

But don't let it. Read over the first few carefully just to get the gist of the features and the language. Then go find some people who know about shopping carts and have opinions about then by simply googling that question or checking them out at forums like Warriorforum.com.

Or you can simply decide on one that look right for you and if you find that their support staff is available only from 9am-5pm or that their server is down too frequently, you can quit and find another.

In our first few years, we tried 3 or maybe 4 until we found the one we have now been with for over 10 years.

All on-line businesses are about getting our messages out to the wide, wild and woolly universe of cyberspace. Without a strategy for delivering the messages we'll have no sales; without sales, we'll be out of business.

Auto-Responder

In my opinion anyone doing email marketing in the twenty-first century must use an auto responder or a list manager. There is no getting around that fact. For an individual to meet the white listing demands of hundreds of internet service providers would in and of itself be a full-time job. And use of a personal ISP for emailing is simply too risky in terms of the potential loss of your ISP due to claims of SPAM.

Both price and capabilities of the systems vary enormously: one can obtain a decent auto responder for less than $10 per month or pay $1200 to $2500 per month. Obviously, the capabilities at the far end of the price far exceed those at the low end. The expensive systems are mostly used by large retail or advertising companies with hundreds of thousands on their mailing lists. The lists are easily segmented by age, gender, purchase history and the like.

Will spending thousands on a list manager guarantee success in marketing?

Unfortunately not.

In spite of all the bells and whistles and choice of templates and segmented population, the copy, frequency and testing must be done by you-unless you can afford to hire an expert.

Auto responder Geeks rank the top three auto responders as AWeber, Get Response and Infusion Soft. All three of these auto responders can be obtained for less than $250.00 per month with AWeber and Get Response at prices of less than $20.00 per month. The methods for deciding which auto responder is best is dictated by budget but it is very important to keep in mind that Auto responder Geeks rank AWeber as the number one-at $19.95 per month.

I have personally used over ten auto responders in the fifteen years that I have been engaged in email marketing and have found that there are only a few ways for me to decide which one will work for me. And they are deliverability, deliverability and deliverability. There are other elements that interest me: the availability and ease of use of templates, the cost per list-if any-, ability to segment the total list and the testing systems for me to determine effects of campaigns. But far and above, my interest is getting the message out and onto email boxes.

Blogging Platforms

Is a blog really essential; in addition to an autoresponder for marketing? A couple of years ago, I'd have said no-maybe even last year. But if you are determined to compete in 2013, a blog is essential.

I read a few weeks ago that there are millions maybe billions of blogs on line and the number is growing daily.

Why?

I think that it fits with this age where everyone wants to give their opinion.

When you have a few minutes, go check out the latest book written by one of your favorite authors and read the reviews by readers.

There are some reviews that are well-written, thoughtful and informative. But if you scan them, you'll find a few or more than a few where the writer of the review is clearly loving giving you his considered opinion—so that's what the people want, we in this crazy, chaotic world of the internet need to give it to them, let them comment all they want.

So should you go with WordPress.com or WordPress.org or Tumblr or even Twitter or Pinterest?

Honestly, I think there is no one answer to that question. I think if I didn't enjoy research and writing, I would have gone with Tumblr rather than Word Press. The best way to find out which method works best for you is to try them and experiment.

A Group of Favored Mentors

We cannot do this alone, we need help from those who did or who are walking in our shoes. If you are in network marketing, you may be lucky and find a real mentor in the man or woman who recruits you into your business but a much more likely scenario is learning that your up-line has flaws as glaring as yours. Rather than allowing this to dampen your enthusiasm and determination to succeed, simply do some on-line research for experts in your field-or far outside your field—who like to write, teach and share their experience, failures and successes.

A couple of my current favored on-line gurus are finance people who love writing about the trials and exhilaration of running their own business, motivating themselves, structuring their time and their energy.

The wisdom available on line is deep and extremely accessible; don't deprive yourself of finding like thinkers.

A Schedule

There is an extensive array of ways to schedule tasks and work. Both the benefit and the burden of working for ourselves is that we are our own boss. For some of us that means that we need discipline to get to the work part and help from someone who knows us well remembering the life part; for others, it is exactly the opposite. I think for all of us the balance between the two is always a tenuous one; I know of no easy answer because like you, I struggle each day with trying to get it right.

An Exercise Routine

Perhaps including an exercise routine in a chapter about merchant accounts, auto responders sounds strange-weird even but I add it because exercise is the only antidote to stress that never fails. And has no side effects.

We home—business owners, independent business owners, on-line marketers, entrepreneurs, work at home moms, network marketers all require fuel (energy) in order to work; or at least to work effectively.

Here's the thing. Running our own home business requires energy: energy to deal with unsatisfied customers charitably, energy to sit down at the computer to meet that deadline we've set for ourselves, energy to go that extra step with a demanding customer, energy to look critically at our business and identify the ways we need to improve. We really need *passion*: passion requires lots of energy.

Many years ago, my life was a mess: my marriage had fallen apart, I was living in the vacant apartment of a generous friend and I had very little money. As I was reflecting on my list of woes one day, I found myself more and more depressed. Suddenly I decided to go for a run with my Doberman. Mind you, I was not a runner, in grade and high school, I had never liked sports, the solo or the team kind. But that day on that first run, do you know what I learned?

The simple act of running occupied my entire mind so completely that I was no longer worrying about my absent husband or my anemic bank book or the fact that I had no idea what I wanted to do with my newly single life. It took all my concentration to focus on putting one foot in front of the other and to wipe the sweat pouring down my face in the hot, humid, Houston Texas climate. I was addicted—I'd found **the** best stress reliever!

CHAPTER SEVEN

LEADS

If a poll were taken of experienced network marketers about lead sources and whether there are "good leads" (people who listen) and "bad leads" (those who hang up when they hear the first few words we say), half of those polled would agree that there are these two categories of leads and half would disagree.

Those who disagree would explain that there are no *bad* leads; there are only bad interviewers. Each of our hypothetical group of experts is right. So let's talk about the bad leads first. It's more fun because we can tell ourselves that it has nothing to do with us. We can blame our inability to build our business on the company that sold us a bunch of bad leads… more fun in the short run that is. But in the end we are the loser because we are out money and time; most of the folks I know in business do not tolerate extremely high business expenses. In fact, if the expenses exceed the income by too much for too long, people quit.

So how can we avoid being one of the members of the first group?

The first way is to become a more intelligent buyer. There is one overriding fact about providers of leads: they do it because it makes them good money. Our job is to do some research and ask questions of the lead source such as, how many other marketers are sold the names?

If possible, verify the answers given by the company with other customers of the company. It is really tough to get the attention of your prospect when ten other networkers are competing with you. It is doubly tough to talk to her if she receives scores of badly written emails promising her thousands next month if she'll join Super MLM Company now. When doing your research on the lead source, find out as much as possible about the methods of advertising as well as the time frame of the response. It is best if the individuals opted in to the source recently, say within a weeks of your purchase of their names.

The more recently one has expressed an interest; the more likely the interest will exist when called.

Another way to assess the leads is to get specific information from the company about the type of ad they use to drive traffic to, and where they are placing their ads. This information is proprietary so don't be surprised if they are unwilling to give you an exact replica of the ad.

The cost of a lead varies from free to over $25.00 per lead. One of the quickest ways to land in the bad leads group is to assume that the higher priced lead means that is better.... not necessarily true. The best and most reliable way to determine the quality of high-priced leads is to buy a small sample of names to begin with and decide for yourself.

How do we avoid becoming a victim of bad lead sources?

The answer is to test the lead source through our own and others' experience. Now why did half of our hypothetical experts say that there no bad leads, only bad interviewers? Remember, we're defining bad leads as those who are unwilling to listen to a presentation; the "close" will be covered later. This is pretty simple and basic stuff but it is remarkable how many of us forget or have never learned.

First, always ask if the prospect has 2-5 minutes (or whatever you need) to talk about the information they have requested. When we call, we want the attention of the person who answers the phone. If they are cooking dinner or watching their favorite show on TV, how likely is it that we will get their attention? Not only is it good business to ask, it is also courteous and courtesy is necessary simply because it is rare.

Remember, it is they who have requested the information so they are not doing you a favor by listening. If you do not believe that to be true, stop wasting your time and money and work with someone who can help you understand this fact. The interview itself must be one that gets attention quickly and focuses immediately on the prospect not on you.

That is an art that requires experience and a lot of feedback. Simply, it is very important to convey an interest in the prospect without allowing distractions.

This can be tough for two reasons.

- First, because we are usually excited and a little nervous when we start to call prospects. So our natural tendency is to talk, not to listen.

- And secondly because most of us in this business like helping people so we can get up with others' sad stories while losing precious time and even more precious energy. Initially interviewing scripts can be extremely helpful. But they are useful only initially because flexibility is very important in order to hear the spoken and unspoken objections in the initial conversation.

Pyramid Objection Answered

One typical objection is the one about pyramid schemes; in my early years as a networker, I thought that people really wanted to know that pyramid schemes are illegal and I would explain the federal law against such schemes. As you may imagine the person at the other end of the phone frequently did not appreciate my "instruction".

So when I hung up the phone, what do you think I thought? Right, bad lead. Now when I hear that objection I have found that the prospect usually throws it out there to let me know that she is skeptical; not because she wants the question or the objection answered directly.

What do we need for the good lead category?

We need the right approach-we need their permission and we need their attention. In the interview we need to stay focused on the fact that they have asked us for the information and we need to control the interview.

Controlling the interview means asking questions and listening for the answers to determine if your business may match what this person is looking for.

And last to identify quickly when it is not and to say good-bye and God bless

CHAPTER EIGHT

BASICS OF TALKING WITH PROSPECTS

There is no secret to the fact that people who build large organizations are people who know how to talk with prospects. Not only do they *know* how but they *like* talking to prospects.

Did they start out that way?

Probably not.

Most of us start out thinking that talking to prospects is different from talking with our friends about the great movie we just saw; the one that was so great that we want everyone to see it. Therefore, when we get started in our brand new business with products we just *know* that everyone we know will love, for the very simple reason that we love them, we freeze when we pick up the phone.

Suddenly the very familiar phone feels like that shoe-phone in *Get Smart*- awkward, huge and foreign. So how do we re-familiarize ourselves with what we have known how to do since we were toddlers?

We mistakenly behave as if it's our *words* which transmit all of the information we need to inform, persuade, excite, or interest another, in this case, our new prospect. And so we memorize scripts, learn all the facts we can about our products, systems and compensation plans in order to recruit more and more people.

At this point, you must be thinking something like this: "Well, of course, we must learn all about our products our systems, how we get paid... how else can we communicate the benefits of our opportunity?"

And you are right, of course, learning those basic facts about your business opportunity is essential. But it's not enough.

Why?

- Studies have shown that people only pay attention to 7% of what is said to them.

- Over 55% of communication occurs via non-verbal methods: body language, facial expression, tone and quality of voice and posture are only some of the non-verbal influencers in communication.

- Silence is one of the most powerful, and underused tools in effective communication.

- We use weak, "wishy washy" language

Weak, "wishy washy" language.

Our listener decides what he or she thinks about our message before our first sentence is out of our mouth.

OK, this is interesting but only for those who are doing face to face marketing not telephone marketing from our home office, right? After all facial expressions, bodily posture cannot be seen by people whom I am speaking with on the phone so this doesn't apply to me.

Wrong.

"Don't think that just because the prospect can't see you, you can slouch down and prop your slippered feet on your computer desk. 'Whatever you do on the phone can be picked up, so have good posture,' says Cheri Kerr, a communications and public speaking coach, owner of ExecuProv, and author of *When I Say This, Do You Mean That?*

Here are 10 simple tips and methods to incorporate into your daily prospecting. See what these fairly minor changes could do to your recruitment.

1. Keep your voice at the low end of its range remembering to speak with volume-this will keep the anxiety and desperation out of your voice.

2. Make your point clearly and concisely. Get rid of extra words which weaken your message.

3. When on the telephone, sit at the edge of your chair, this will automatically straighten your back.

4. After you have made your point, stop talking. Learn to make use of silence, to consider it your friend—it means your prospect is thinking.

5. Bring passion into your voice. If you don't have it, fake it.

6. Rehearse

7. Stay away from jargon

8. Lead with statements that everyone would agree with

9. Speak simply

10. Give small nuggets of information

Rehearse

Come up with a script that works for you, feels like *your* words and not those of your up-line, words that you *believe* are true and get comfortable with it. Walk around the house practicing, take it with you while you walk the dog and practice. Until it flows, feels like part of you.

Then try it on your wife or husband or dog.

Careful though, you want to sound natural, not as if you're reading a script so try not to memorize.

Stay Away From Jargon

Although it may not seem so to you, the vocabulary of network marketing is unique. Words and phrases like up-line, down-line, comp plan and even residual income are concepts not understood by people not in the industry.

So don't use those terms, explain what you need to using plain language.

Lead with statements that everyone would agree with.

The best way to begin a relationship with a person and never forget, that is what we do here, we work to build relationships, is to begin the conversation with statements that almost everyone would agree with.

Statements like, "Working for ourselves sure beats working for the corporation, doesn't it?"

Or, " When you average out the cost of commuting to a job in terms of gas, wear and tear on the car and clothing, there really isn't any comparison, is there?"

The agreement with statements like this helps lead your conversation toward your prospect considering what this might be like for him or for her and helps get the two of you on the same page.

Speak simply

Speaking is very similar to writing: the best words are the simplest. Words that pack a punch, that are clearly understood and visualized, word pictures. Stay away from complicated or fancy terminology.

Give small nuggets of information

One of the biggest mistakes we make when learning how to talk with our customer is "TMI", too much information. We want to tell them about the FDA approval, the scientific studies backing up our products, the unique benefit of our compensation plan. And we totally lose our prospect in all of our chatter.

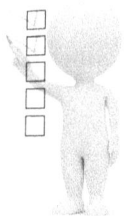

CHAPTER NINE

HANDLING OBJECTIONS AKA THE CLOSE

After working with hundreds of recruits in three different businesses, I learned that most people cannot close. And I think there are three very simple answers to why that is a fact. And it *is* a fact.

The average network marketer recruits two to three people (often family members recruited by their up-line). And when they quit they do it because they are not making the money they expected to make or they are spending too much money or...But in reality, most never start.

It doesn't have to be this way. Here are the three reasons why:

1. We overcomplicate the whole process
2. We think we're not selling
3. Because we think we don't sell, we don't learn how

Making the Process Complicated

Let's start with the process. Joining my first company was a familiar and very comfortable process for me... It felt as if I were back in school. Immediately I bought all the training materials: lots of books, audiotapes and videotapes.

I used all the techniques that my up-line suggested and generally "went by the book(s)". And I taught everyone else to do exactly what I did.

But no one recruited more than two to three people. Most recruited no one.

No experience is wasted but those first two years make me sad for only one reason. I recruited many people who could have made a little–or a lot–of money doing the business had I not made it so complicated.

So if it doesn't need to be this complicated, what should we do?

I'm Not Selling

We realize that we *are* selling!

And we decide to get good, really good at looking for and listening to people who will fit with our business… (otherwise known as selling).

When I joined my first network marketing company over 17 years ago, I was told this was not selling. Worse yet, I taught everyone I recruited that it was not sales…we were all "professionals" and somehow "above" sales.

Once I figured out that sales was nothing like what I thought it was I began to close even more folks with a lot less work. But it was too late for the down-line that I had taught to rely on me.

Learning How to Sell

If you are like most people, then the word "sales" strikes fear, disgust, repulsion or all three in your heart.

The perspiring hand, over-eager, often aggressive attitude and air of desperation combine to make people of most walks of life shudder at the thought of it… of referring to oneself as a salesman.

And yet why was the Internet jam-packed with eulogies to Zig Ziglar when he died? And why did some of the biggest names of the Internet refer to him with a reverence approaching awe?

For what was Ziglar best known for? Right that dreaded "sales" word we love to hate.

Overcoming prejudice

The prejudice against selling is like every other: It is based on ignorance. And in this case, an ignorance created by literary giants like Arthur Miller when he portrayed Willy Loman as a grasping, rather despicable and desperate man.

Arthur Miller won a Pulitzer for his play *Death of a Salesman*. Decades later, playwright David Mamet won a Pulitzer for *Glengarry Glen Rose*, another tale of desperate people spouting dialogue such as this:

> *Because only one thing counts in this life: Get them to sign on the line which is dotted. You hear me you...? A-B-C. A-Always, B-Be, C-Closing. Always be closing. ALWAYS BE CLOSING. A-I-D-A. Attention, Interest, Decision, Action. Attention - Do I have your attention? Interest - Are you interested?*

Not very long ago, many of us were glued to our television to see who was the better leader, Obama or Romney. We have different words for what they were doing: charisma, oratorical ability, eloquence but each man was trying to persuade us, *move* us, convince us. And that is the heart of it.

You do it and I do it each and every day in which we put forth our opinion, when we write or tell someone about a book we loved and want them to read. But more importantly, if we are in business we had better become experts in leaning what our customers are looking for and give them more.

Fear of Objection

These are some very practical tips that have been extremely useful for me.

1. *The fact that objections mean a high level of interest.*
2. *The spoken objections are not the real ones.*
3. *Most people need the decision made for them.*

If a prospect is not interested they will not expend the time or the energy to put up objections.

Many of us fear the objections and believe that our explanation to each objection is important-critically important.

Not so.

It took me many useless verbal rabbit trails to learn the wisdom of asking this question before I answered any of the spoken objections:

> "Ms. Prospect, if we are able to agree that company xyz is not a pyramid scheme and that your understanding of sales can be changed

to a process that you would consider fun, are there any other factors keeping you from making this decision?"

Always, out it would come…. "my husband", "other people's opinions" etc. When I remembered to use this question, there was never any need to discuss all the others put out there to confuse both the prospect and me.

Ask for the Close

The third and maybe most critical step is: *People will not close themselves.*

This is so critical that it bears repeating, and in bold:

People will not close themselves.

We must learn to ask for the close. How do you do it?

By asking.

Once you begin you will be amazed at how many folks will quite amicably provide the information that you need for your enrollment process.

> "Ms Prospect, we've discussed your interest in XY and Z. And, Ms Prospect, we've discussed the low risk nature of this decision."

(This is NOT a big deal, right?)

> "Now let's see Ms Prospect, How do you spell your first name?"

Even if you know how to spell her name, ask her to spell it for you, it will relieve her anxiety because she is in control. This part is critical. Stay focused.

The worst case? They say "no" or "I need to know *this* or *that*" or "no I don't think this is right for me."

But in either case you win because you have saved yourself time.

Summary

Decide *today* to:

1. simplify your process,
2. study sales techniques and
3. do a trial close on your very next prospect

CHAPTER TEN

A WORD OR THREE
ABOUT UNHAPPY CUSTOMERS

Irate customers are a fact of life for each of us if we seek to offer something- anything, to others. Given that fact, what do we do with the few but memorable customers who are unhappy, even enraged by what they have purchased from us?

If you do a search on this subject, you'll find a lot of articles written by writers or marketers about the best way to handle hostile readers or consumers. Many will advise that we ignore the person by refusing to be drawn in to an unwinnable conversation.

But I believe there is no choice but to respond and to do so immediately.

Why?

I have several reasons. My first requires that we place ourselves in the shoes of our furious customer.

- Consider how you feel once you have taken the time to call or compose a complaint to the company or individual with whom you are unhappy. You expect a response, generally right away, don't you?

- If you receive only silence from a written complaint or superficial excuses from the person answering the phone, is it likely that you will you forget it and move on? Probably not.

- Once the steps of generating the energy for writing or calling with the complaint, you are physiologically wired for action- if you get none, you'll ramp up your actions, whether it is asking for a supervisor, calling your credit card company to initiate a dispute so that you can rescind payment, you'll do something to dissipate all that energy.

- Once the next steps have been accomplished, there is often sufficiently abundant negative energy remaining for you to talk about your experience on Twitter, Face Book and any other social media you participate in.

That's why I advise dealing with the angry customer and immediately. Although it is very tempting to ignore the person and to engage in "normal" activities, you'll be carrying that person's anger around with you even if you pretend to ignore her.

But you know you can't do it, you'll keep thinking about all that emotion… directed at you.

So my strong suggestion?

Deal with it and get rid of all that energy; yours and hers.

The following 6 steps are some methods I have learned over the years that work each and every time; the only time they have not are when I forget to do the first step.

1. Listen. Experience will teach you how to handle the most hostile of customers with almost no exceptions, beginning with that magic word listen and plenty of practice will enable you to do so without reacting.
2. When the phone rings, and an angry person is at the other end, simply listen.

My desk is situated such that I can look out a large window out into my yard. So rather than reacting to the anger or the criticism; I look out at the sky and the birds until she exhausts herself.

1. Don't disagree. Our natural tendency is to defend our product, never do that, it will simply re-invest the customer with the belief that she must convince you that she is right.
2. Ask her what she would like you to do about this. This is critical because you may think you know what they want but frequently, you'll be very surprised at the response.

3. Violate your policy. If you have a policy of no refunds, give one, if you don't give replacements for free, replace her product-for free.

4. If the request is completely totally unreasonable, answer truthfully-always truthfully. For example, "sure we can do that but I don't think you would like what I would have to charge you for… and repeat the completely absurd demand.

5. Over time, you'll be able to convert almost all of your most hostile to your most loyal customers once you decide to do so and you'll also be surprised at the effect of your new skills on your spouse, kids and friends.

But there are times when the most skilled, patient series of replies will not help and rare times when a response from you may simply ignite a smoldering flame.

- When the content of the criticism is intentionally destructive. A customer who engages in emotional tirades replete with ridicule, rage and invective may well be someone whom it is best to ignore, particularly if you're not experienced in dealing with hostility.

- Ignoring intensely personal criticism may be wise for those newly engaged in their business or in their writing simply because we need enormous energy and hope when we are starting something new and fundamentally risky, allowing the negative opinions of others to penetrate the psyche of new entrepreneur may be enough to stop him in his tracks.

- If the content of the complaint is clearly incorrect and worded such that the writer is more interested in demonstrating his own expertise than in an accurate reading of what you have written, probably it is best to avoid an argument.

CHAPTER ELEVEN
FUNDAMENTALS OF WRITING GOOD COPY

If the idea of sitting at a computer to write makes you sweat bullets, consider a serious illness to avoid it or any of the other variety of "...I can't write" phobias, this chapter is for you!

I believe in short, practical and simple copy: so I'll cover the 14 most critical steps in writing copy, for your ads and for your emails.

Before I give you the list, however, let me dispel just a few myths.

Myths

The more you tell the more you sell.

This is one of my favorites. Like all myths there is some truth there. The truth is that if you write about something that excites the reader, a topic they are really interested in, that is true. But if you write about what you and what excites you, will that excite your reader?

Probably not.

Know the Facts

Yes, there are some analytical types who do "know the facts" but never forget that most buying decisions are made in the unconscious mind.

So emotion is **good,** not bad. The most powerful copy is a blend of logic and emotion or "right and left brain".

Money

Do not assume that the number one reason to buy is about money. It is usually something else: maybe achievement, security, self-improvement, status, style… just to name a few. Money is generally at the end of the list.

Fourteen critical steps for writing "power" copy

1. Know your Competition

Begin by reading through 50 or 100 of the business op emails that you receive in your e-mail box. These emails show you what your competition is and show you that you can beat it!

You'll find that the messages you read, on average, will be: full of hype (promising big money in a few weeks) crammed full of features (all kinds of facts about the company and how stable it is, the president and how brilliant he is etc.) And you'll find that none or very, very few will tell you clearly *what is in it for you?* In short, you will find the reading boring and tedious…spam!

2. Write

Now start writing. Stop making excuses, just sit down and do it. Now that you know what *not* to do.

Very important. Pick a fairly simple first message and just start to write it. Many email marketing campaigns fall flat because they don't clearly convey the benefit. To get to where you need to be, you'll write several revisions. This is a good thing—honest.

Ask the pros and they will tell you that they revise and revise and then change their message again.

Leave it alone for a day or three. Then come back to it, remembering how you felt when you were reading those boring, tedious 100 emails about how you could become a millionaire by Christmas.

3. Revise

Revise what you've written so that it fits what seems to work best in email marketing: short, punchy, action oriented and evocative.

These are so very important, we'll go through each of them one by one, backwards.

4. Use Power Words

Use evocative words and phrases or more precisely "power words" in your message.

Example 1

Think of yourself when you look at an ad for a steak: which grabs you more; "delicious" or "mouth watering"?

Doesn't *mouth-watering* appeal to you more than *delicious* if you think of your favorite cut of steak?

Mouth watering *evokes*…causes…a salivation response in you, doesn't it? (If you like steak, that is.) It is as if you can cut it with a fork.

That's what you want your email message to do…cause your recipient to picture, taste, smell, and see.

Example 2

Say that you are explaining how the commission structure works for your business. Which of these 2 explanations do you like better?

> "Recruit just three friends and you get your service for free!"

That's ok but this is better, isn't it?:

> "The last time that three of your friends went to see a movie that you recommended, did the theater *pay* you for the referrals?
>
> And did you get a percentage of the popcorn they bought?"

The reader gets a **very** clear picture of the benefit to her.

According to Jay Levinson, the "Guerilla Marketing" guru, most advertising campaigns fail due to a failure to communicate the benefits clearly and concisely.

5. Use Action-oriented copy

Action oriented simply means that your message impels your recipient to act:

because your offer will expire in three days,

because your free report is offered only to the first 30 or 100 customers.

Be sure to mean it though…most Internet readers are pretty savvy.

So if they see that same message from you that will expire in 3 days a month from now, they will most likely notice.

6. Copy with a Punch

What is punchy? Let's start with what's not.

Here is an example of "non-punchy" (boring, uninteresting)

> "These products are approved by the Federal Drug Administration. The FDA is an agency of the federal government to oversee the effectiveness and efficacy of pharmaceuticals manufactured in the US…"

A few will want to read that so put the information in a link so they can access it. Most will not be interested.

> "Our products are safe (link), guaranteed and will work for you. See how Sharon Adams looked before she lost 100 pounds with product X."

Almost punchy but can be improved.

7. Keep it Short

The length of advertising copy is a subject of some debate. Some say that short is always better; others claim (with data) that longer copy results in a higher percentage of purchase decisions. If your copy is clear, exciting and compelling, most will read it—*long* or *short*.

We tend to favor short copy simply because our product is not complicated.

8. Testimonials

Remember: You are appealing to an audience that wants prestige either because they want to be thinner than their neighbor or because they want a bigger house, or car, or…Testimonials are extremely powerful…with pictures and or audio, even more so.

9. Our customer is looking for us to solve a problem: To relieve their pain.

Our problem then becomes one of identifying the problem for our customer. She may think she knows what she wants but she has not thought deeply enough to get underneath what she thinks she hates to talk about what she loves. For example, a woman who believes that she is looking for an on-line business may be looking for friends, for people with whom she has something in common.

10. Be Unique

Make your headlines and your copy unique.

Use phrases that stick like "as jam packed with ways for you to save time as a Reuben sandwich" or" your new body, as sleek as a jaguar"

11. Follow-up

Follow up, over and over and over. Do not make the mistake of mailing only once!

12. Make the headline "pop"

Remember your headline; it is **the** most critical part of your message. It is what the readers see first, so make it entice them to read the rest of the message.

13. Both-Brain copy

Use language that appeals to left-brained *and* right-brained folks

14. Price is NOT an issue.

Do not forget that for over 60% of folks, price is not the issue.

CHAPTER TWELVE

Sounding Professional In your Emails

Sounding professional in emails is no different from sounding professional in writing proposals, business communications or any other type of formal communication.

There are three basic fundamentals of writing which cannot be compromised:

- spelling,
- coherence, and
- clarity.

Typographical errors

Spelling errors serve as red flags in email communication: nothing conveys carelessness and unprofessionalism like poor spelling.

When we see a misspelled word, most readers frequently make negative judgments about the knowledge and capability of the writer. It can take only one misspelled word to evoke the critic in all of us

Although there are innumerable aids to spelling available through software programs like word, the numbers of folks who make spelling errors in their every day communication in emails is astounding.

Even with spell check, errors in word usage and context may pass the spell check but be grammatically incorrect. Those who have little experience in writing and or are poor spellers would do well to ask someone to proofread their messages before sending them.

An incoherent email message will end your message in the trash.

How to Avoid being Incoherent

Once more there are a few fundamentals that are universal:

- Organize your thoughts. Stop to consider exactly what you are attempting to communicate.

- Are you selling?

- Are you informing?

- Are you seeking information?

Consider using some type of organizational aid for your thoughts.

- If you are new to writing formally, use a written outline beginning with the major then supporting points of your message.

- Others may do well with a verbal outline such as I used in the beginning of this article: spelling, coherence and clarity.

- Be concise; once you have made your point, move on.

- Proof read your message or your article not just once but several times.

- When you write, use words that you know and have used before. Don't trap yourself by using words to impress but that you run the risk of using incorrectly.

Clarity is critical in email marketing both for the obvious reason of the need to be understood but also because most people scan articles. They are busy and are looking for the important nuggets of information to digest easily.

- If you are writing informational material, the use of lists enhances the ability of your reader to distill the essential information out of your piece and move on.

- If you are writing sales copy, the same principle holds true.

- The benefits of the product or program must be clearly conveyed and the offer must be prominently displayed in the message.

So how do we sound more professional in our email messages?

1. We assure that all words are spelled correctly.
2. We write in an organized manner and make our points simply.
3. The subject matter of our message is crystal clear.

CHAPTER THIRTEEN

DRIVING TRAFFIC TO YOUR SITE

If you have a website that's still struggling to generate targeted leads, attract customers or subscribers and even the trickle of leads that you get don't convert to sales, you are probably using marketing strategies that are outdated and no longer work.

When social media hit the Internet marketing scene, the large companies were quick on the uptake as they saw the opportunity to diversify their marketing efforts to reach millions of people in an expanding global market using carefully engineered social media marketing campaigns.

Even though traditional methods for prospecting for new customers will always be important, they are not as effective anymore and cannot be relied on exclusively. Social media enables businesses and consumers to interact far more effectively than even email.

Sneak Peek of New Products

Offering a sneak preview of new products, services, or features online can help build demand and provide critical feedback to help smooth the launch.

Viral Videos

Chances are your company's white paper won't go viral. But sharing knowledge you've gathered through your trade can go a long way toward boosting your brand. Ford Models, for instance, became a YouTube sensation through a series of videos that featured its models giving beauty and fashion tips.

Because multimedia is so integral to social media, getting connected allows you to express your company's value proposition beyond words. To show just how powerful his company's blenders were, Blendtec's head of marketing, George Wright, created a series of videos showing the appliances churning up such diverse items as a rotisserie chicken, a Rubik's Cube, and an iPhone. The series' 100 million combined views helped boost Blendtec's sales by 700 percent.

Encourage Content Sharing

Want to draw more traffic to your website? Help spread the word by encouraging visitors to share content they enjoy. GotCast, a website that connects television casting directors with aspiring actors, draws new visitors by posting audition videos on Digg and allowing others to share video links on the site. One way to promote the sharing of your site's content is to install a widget, such as AddThis, that automates linking to popular sites.

Participate

Just putting up a blog or a Facebook fan page won't do much good if visitors sense the flow of conversation only goes one way. In fact, Matt Mullenweg, founder of blogging platform WordPress, lists not participating in comments as a surefire way to kill a community. Mullenweg and his team field the many suggestions users have for WordPress through his blog.

Preparation

With 800 million users on Facebook, 200 million on Twitter and other networks also booming, the potential to find new customers via social media has never been greater. Whether you're already up and running or a novice, the experts say the crucial thing is to prepare carefully and do it right.

It's understandable that many companies are yet to take full advantage of social media – so say the experts at research consultancy TNS, who recently completed a survey of more than 72,000 consumers in 60 countries and concluded that brands are losing time and money online with ineffective social media strategies.

> "Social media is still a relatively new phenomenon in terms of its mass-market adoption," says chief development officer Matthew Froggatt. "So companies not having their stuff together in this area is excusable.

Time Commitment

An interesting, regularly updated social media presence from the leader of a business can really impress potential customers. Many chief executives are deterred by the perceived time commitment, but Twitter, Facebook and Google+ user Sir Richard Branson says it's not such a chore. "It's not that hard to do," he says. "It's fun to share what I'm doing and who I'm with – be it at a Carbon War Room meeting with climate wealth entrepreneurs, the Grand Prix with Rihanna, checking out Virgin Galactic space vehicles with future astronauts or raising money for the London Marathon."

Once you open up a channel of social media interaction, consistently responding to any correspondence received is essential, and can impress existing and potential customers. A survey by Mr Youth, a New York-based marketing agency specializing in social media, found that brands using social networking are responding to only 61 per cent of inquiries made on their Twitter accounts, and 55 per cent of inquiries on Facebook – and yet conversions to purchase have reached as high as 80 per cent when potential customers received a response.

> "On the one hand there's the chance to respond quickly when an answer is demanded, to demonstrate you're listening and you care," says Froggatt. "But then there's also the opportunity, when there's less expectation of a rapid response, to surprise and delight with a message which demonstrates that the brand is out there, alive and being sociable."

Social media marketing is taking the business world by storm. If you have spent even a little time building your business online you would have heard from the marketing gurus that social media for your business is a skill that you must master to be successful in the new economy. If you're lost about taking the next step in Marketing Online Successfully – then Social Media is the most effective marketing tool to help you dominate your market.

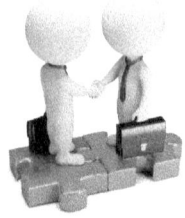

CHAPTER FOURTEEN
CONVERTING TRAFFIC TO CUSTOMERS

The point of search engine optimization or SEO, of keywords which rank very high in the search engines, Google, Yahoo and Bing, of making sure that our landing pages have the proper number and properly placed Meta tags is to generate traffic to our websites, right?

No, that's not the point.

I can hear you arguing with me right now as you read this, shaking your head in disbelief; "What is she talking about?" You're mumbling to yourself, "*of course* I need a boatload of traffic going to my website, how else am I going to make the sale?"

But see, here's the thing: traffic can cost you a boatload of money without generating any sales and that fact can redden your bottom line faster than the traditional speeding bullet.

Search terms, especially in our business of Internet marketing have doubled, some have tripled and a few are four times more expensive in 2013 than they were even 3 years ago at Google. MLM, work at home, network marketing search terms were once under a dollar, now they may cost you as much as 4 dollars at Google.

Even online, we are a society of window shoppers. On average, a measly three percent of visitors to a company's website make a purchase or fork over contact information, says Chris Golec, CEO of Demandbase, a Web-based lead-generation service. Our task is to determine ways to target the 3% who are interested in what we offer.

Finding Targeted Traffic

The first step is to find a tool so that we can spend time looking at those who are looking at us. Google Analytics can help with this but a small investment in Go Clicky can provide a wide array of who is visiting your site and how long they are staying; critical information.

Keywords

If you find that you have a large amount of traffic which stays on your site for only seconds and then leaves, you can infer that your key words are attracting people looking for something other than what you are selling and you can experiment with more specific key words.

Content

Relevant content will result in someone staying on your site simply because they find the material you are offering interesting. The longer they stay on your site, the more likely are they to take action.

Location

Surprisingly, people need very clear direction to take action. If you find, for example, that visitors are on your site for over a minute but are not buying, clicking on your free product or taking the action you want them to take, you may need to move your sign up box, or be more directive on your page, like 'download now' or 'buy now and save 20%."

Relationship

The key to conversion is the establishment of a relationship with the visitor who will become a customer. Offering a free E-Book about something relevant to your product can be quite compelling.

Engaging the visitor in conversation through offering a 1-800 number or a chat window can frequently result in a purchase. In this cyber world of anonymity, there is no more powerful sales tool than you and your knowledge.

CHAPTER FIFTEEN

SUMMARY

I heard about the work-life or time-money formulas about 15 years ago when I made the leap from corporate career to working for myself. I can recall sitting in the audience as the presenter made his point.

Either we have money and no time (insert work and no life) or we have time and no money. I have no idea how anyone else in the audience received the speaker's simple statement but I was floored. Put like that, I had to accept that my life prior to that evening had been work…somehow all of the warnings from friends and family during those years had been like water off of a duck's back. But sitting there, listening to that speaker on that night, I got what those who loved me had been telling me for years.

Looking back, I don't regret the years consumed by work, writing, publishing and study but I admit that I occasionally wonder what my life would had been like if I'd not been so driven. And now, all these years later, I find that I am still struggling to achieve the balance between life and work. Balance does not come easy.

I remember when I became a Christian Catholic; one of my first spiritual directors told me that "we are all redeemed sinners but that half of us emphasize the redeemed part of the equation to the exclusion of the sinner while the other half focused on the second half". He smiled kindly at me as he said that converts tended to fall into the second group.

So working at home for ourselves is like that; it is a balance, and a very delicate one at that. Trying to make sure that we work hard enough to make the money we need but not so hard that we miss the life going on, with or without us.

ABOUT DR. LIN WILDER

I spent most of my life working at work and in school. Once I reached Hospital Director at a major academic medical center in New England and completed a doctorate in Public Health, I began wondering if there may be another way to live.

Fifteen years later, I wonder why it took me so long to learn that working for myself is far superior to working for another.

I have always loved to write and have published extensively in the fields of cardiovascular physiology, hospital administration and general management. And later when I converted to Catholic Christianity, I began to write for Catholic women's magazines on a variety of subjects.

I continue to love writing-especially about the challenges involved in working from home and all that the phrase entails: dealing with skeptical friends and relatives, developing a system to manage ourselves, how to self-motivate and avoiding some of the pitfalls of being a new business owner.

I have become quite passionate about the benefits of working from home and have decided recently to ramp up my writing in hopes that some of what I write may be useful to others looking for a better way to live without sacrificing a reasonable income.

Follow Lin Wilder at:

LinWilder.com
FastMLMLeads.com
Lleads.com
http://www.amazon.com/Dr.-Lin-Wilder/e/B007L380OM/

www.ingramcontent.com/pod-product-compliance
Lightning Source LLC
Chambersburg PA
CBHW071809170526
45167CB00003B/1237